CULTURE IN ACTION

Beyoncé

A LIFE IN MUSIC

Mary Colson

Chicago, Illinois

www.heinemannraintree.com

Visit our website to find out more information about Heinemann-Raintree books.

To order:

☎ Phone 888-454-2279

💻 Visit www.heinemannraintree.com to browse our catalog and order online.

Edited by Louise Galpine and Diyan Leake
Designed by Victoria Allen
Original illustrations © Capstone Global Library Ltd 2011
Illustrated by Randy Schirz
Picture research by Hannah Taylor

Originated by Capstone Global Library Ltd
Printed in and bound in China by CTPS

14 13 12 11 10
10 9 8 7 6 5 4 3 2 1

Library of Congress Cataloging-in-Publication Data
Colson, Mary.
  Beyonce : a life in music / Mary Colson.
      p. cm. -- (Culture in action)
  Includes bibliographical references and index.
  ISBN 978-1-4109-3914-2 (hc)
  1. Beyoncé, 1981---Juvenile literature. 2. Singers--United States--Biography--Juvenile literature. I. Title.
  ML3930.K66C65 2011
  782.42164092--dc22
  [B]
                            2009052579

Acknowledgments
The author and publishers are grateful to the following for permission to reproduce copyright material: Corbis pp. **5** (Reuters/Rick Wilking), **7** (Reuters/Lucas Jackson), **26** (epa/Rainer Jensen), **27** (Reuters/Eric Gaillard); Getty Images pp. **6** (WireImage/Arnold Turner), **11** (WireImage/Jim Smeal), **14** (AFP/Toru Yamanaka), **17** (Frank Micelotta), **18** (Alphonso Chan), **21** (Kevin Winter), **22** (WireImage/James Devaney); Photolibrary p. **20**; Reuters pp. **4** (Mario Anzuoni), **12**, **13** (Sam Mircovich), **24** (Molly Riley), **25** (Mike Hutchings); Rex Features pp. **8** (David Fisher), **10** (Everett Collection), **16** (Peter Brooker), **23** (John Rahim).

Cover photograph of Beyoncé at the 40th NAACP Image Awards on February 12, 2009, in Los Angeles, California, reproduced with permission of Getty Images (WireImage/Kevin Parry).

We would like to thank Jackie Murphy for her invaluable help in the preparation of this book.

Every effort has been made to contact copyright holders of any material reproduced in this book. Any omissions will be rectified in subsequent printings if notice is given to the publisher.

Disclaimer
All the Internet addresses (URLs) given in this book were valid at the time of going to press. However, due to the dynamic nature of the Internet, some addresses may have changed, or sites may have changed or ceased to exist since publication. While the author and publisher regret any inconvenience this may cause readers, no responsibility for any such changes can be accepted by either the author or the publisher.

Author
Mary Colson is an experienced teacher and writer of non-fiction books for children. She has too many favorite Beyoncé songs to choose just one favorite!

Literacy consultant
Jackie Murphy is Director of Arts at the Center of Teaching and Learning, Northeastern Illinois University. She works with teachers, artists, and school leaders internationally.

Contents

Some words are printed in bold, **like this**. You can find out what they mean by looking in the glossary on page 30.

Who Is Beyoncé?

Some people are so famous they only need to use one name. Beyoncé is an entertainment **icon**: award-winning singer, dancer, songwriter, actress, model, and businesswoman. With over 100 million records sold over her career, Beyoncé is a role model to many people who admire her musical talent and style.

Spectacular performer

Shy by nature, Beyoncé says that she feels "at home" on the stage. Beyoncé's stage outfits are very **flamboyant**. Her live shows are dazzling displays of music, dance, and **choreography**. The *I Am …* tour employed ten musicians, three backing singers, and a whole crew of dancers.

Beyoncé gets her unusual first name from her mother's family name of Beyincé.

Campaigner

After Hurricane Katrina devastated New Orleans, Louisiana, in 2005, Beyoncé and fellow Destiny's Child singer Kelly Rowland set up a charity. The Survivor Foundation helped organize temporary housing for people who had lost their homes in the storm.

Fashion icon

Image is very important in the entertainment industry. Many people want to copy Beyoncé's look. Beyoncé and her mother set up their House of Deréon fashion label in 2004, adding a line for younger girls in 2006. Beyoncé and her sister, Solange, model for the collection. Beyoncé also appears in advertisements for makeup and perfume.

Actress

Like two of her musical idols, Barbra Streisand and Diana Ross, Beyoncé has moved into acting and has already won praise for her movie performances. She has starred in the movie *Cadillac Records*, in which she played singer Etta James. The song "At Last," which Beyoncé performed at President Barack Obama's **inauguration**, was one of Etta James's songs.

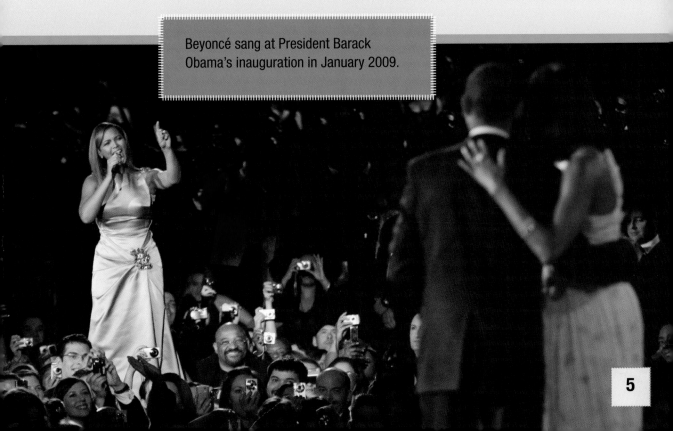

Beyoncé sang at President Barack Obama's inauguration in January 2009.

Early Life

Beyoncé Giselle Knowles was born on September 4, 1981. Her tight-knit family lived in Houston, Texas. Her mother, Tina, was a hair stylist, and her father, Mathew, was a medical equipment salesperson. Today, they are her stylist and manager. Beyoncé's sister, Solange, is also a singer and actress.

A musical education

From an early age, Beyoncé took dance classes in ballet and jazz. She also attended various **performing arts** schools. In 1990 she went to Parker Elementary School, a school specializing in music in Houston, where she joined the school choir. Always singing, today Beyoncé says that she sings Whitney Houston songs in the shower!

Beyoncé's family is very important to her. Here she is with her sister, Solange, and parents, Tina and Mathew Knowles.

Beyoncé and Justin Timberlake did not win on the talent show *Star Search* when they were young, but they went on to be successful and to sing together in concerts, like this one in 2008.

Girl's Tyme

At the age of nine, Beyoncé and her friend Kelly Rowland **auditioned** for places in a girl group. They passed and joined Girl's Tyme along with four other girls: LaTavia Roberson, Támar Davis, and sisters Nikki and Nina Taylor. Dancing and rapping, they had their first national television appearance in 1992 on a television show called *Star Search*, which searched for the country's best new talent.

In good company

Lots of today's stars went on *Star Search* when they were younger. Girl's Tyme did not win, but neither did Britney Spears, Justin Timberlake, nor Christina Aguilera when they competed. Beyoncé has said that this failure made her very driven to succeed.

Living with Beyoncé

Kelly Rowland's mother worked as a live-in nanny for another family. She was not able to get Kelly to rehearsals easily, so Kelly went to live with Beyoncé's family.

Search for a Star

In 1993 three members of Girl's Tyme left the group. LeToya Luckett joined Beyoncé, Kelly Rowland, and LaTavia Roberson. The group needed a new name. After experimenting with different ideas, Tina Knowles looked in her Bible one day and saw the word "destiny." Destiny's Child was born.

Two years later, Mathew Knowles resigned from his job in order to manage the group full time. He created a tough **regime** for the group, and the girls rehearsed their singing and dance routines every day. Tina was in charge of their image, creating ideas for their clothes and hair. Beyoncé has said that her busy childhood did not allow her to have many friends.

Striving for success

Totally committed to success, LaTavia, Kelly, Beyoncé, and LeToya (from left to right in the photo) sang everywhere—at churches, store openings, and as the **opening act** for bigger bands. Sadly, all the pressure and focus on the group contributed to Beyoncé's parents' decision to separate.

Performance activity

Destiny's Child rehearsed its dance routines until they were perfect.

Steps to follow:

1. With two friends, choose a song that has a strong beat to it.

2. Think about how and where you will stand when the music starts.

3. Work with the music to create a series of dance steps. Try to create patterns and interesting shapes by moving in different directions.

4. Remember to use your face when you dance! Using expressions and body language will help to communicate your dance's attitude.

5. Think about the outline your body will have in different positions.

6. When the chorus plays, always do the same steps. This will make your performance hold together.

7. When you perform your dance, remember to hold your head up, face your audience, and be confident.

Destined for Fame

Desperate to get a recording **contract**, Destiny's Child performed at concerts all over Houston and **auditioned** for record companies at the same time. The group was signed to Elektra Records in 1995, but was dropped a few months later. When a record company or label "signs" an artist, it means that the artist is employed by the label. If the record does not sell well, the artist is "dropped" and does not record with that label anymore.

What is R&B?

R&B, or rhythm and blues, is a type of music first created by African American musicians in the 1940s and 1950s. It covers a wide range of music, including soul, gospel, and pop. Famous R&B artists include Whitney Houston and Jennifer Lopez (right). Known to her fans as J-Lo, Jennifer Lopez has sold nearly 50 million albums worldwide. Like Beyoncé, she has a successful fashion business as well as a perfume line and an acting career.

In late 1997, the group was signed to Columbia Records. Columbia also worked with artists such as Mariah Carey and Alicia Keys. Beyoncé still records for Columbia today. One of the first songs the group recorded was "Killing Time." This was on the **soundtrack** to the 1997 Will Smith movie *Men in Black*.

Record rewards

In 1998 the group released its first album, called *Destiny's Child*. The first hit single was "No, No, No." The group won three Soul Train Lady of Soul Awards that year, including the award for Best R&B/Soul Album of the Year.

Destiny's Child won at the 1998 Soul Train Lady of Soul Awards.

The writing's on the wall

In 1999 the group hit the big time with its album called *The Writing's on the Wall*. It sold more than 11 million copies worldwide. One of the songs, "Say My Name," was a global hit and became one of the group's **signature songs**.

The Writing's on the Wall album won two Grammy Awards in 2001. The Grammy Awards are the music industry's Oscars.

Precious metal music

In the music industry, artists win prizes for high record sales. Precious metals are used for the prizes, kind of like Olympic medals. To win a gold record, a single or album has to sell 500,000 copies. To win a platinum award, a million copies have to be sold. The highest prize is the multi-platinum award, for two million copies sold. Over the group's career, Destiny's Child won many gold and platinum records. As a solo artist, Beyoncé has won even more, including several multi-platinum records.

In 2000 Destiny's Child's song "Independent Woman Part I" was used on the *Charlie's Angels* movie soundtrack. It went to number one on the U.S. music charts and on other charts around the world. In the photo above, the new group lineup of Kelly Rowland, Beyoncé, and Michelle Williams pose with the Grammy Awards they won in 2001.

A difficult destiny

Diana Ross is one of Beyoncé's idols (see box on page 21). Like Ross's 1960s group, The Supremes, Destiny's Child also changed its members. LeToya Luckett and LaTavia Roberson both left the group in 2000 due to arguments, disagreements, and the threat of a court case for **breach of contract**. When LeToya and LaTavia left, Farrah Franklin and Michelle Williams joined. Farrah Franklin was with the group for only five months, but Michelle Williams stayed. The new Destiny's Child lineup was set.

Surviving the split

The group's third album, *Survivor*, went multi-platinum around the world. It went straight to number one on the album charts in the United States, the United Kingdom, and Canada, and it was in the top 10 across Europe. One of the hit singles was "Bootylicious." The songs on the album are, in part, about the breakup of the original group.

LeToya Luckett and LaTavia Roberson were upset by the content of the songs on the album and thought they were being personally attacked. They started legal proceedings again, but the case was eventually settled out of court. LeToya became a successful solo artist and LaTavia also started recording again.

Destiny's Child's success around the world meant the members could get involved in charities worldwide. Here they are visiting a child in a hospital in Japan.

Rap writing

Beyoncé is influenced by rap music. A rap is spoken poetry set to a musical beat. It is a powerful way of expressing yourself.

Write a 16-line rap to introduce yourself and perform it for your friends.

Steps to follow:

1. Find some music with a strong, regular beat. Play this in the background as you rap.

2. Using "My name is ..." as a starting line, think of an adjective to describe yourself. Try to make it rhyme with your name—for example, "My name is Mary. I'm not so scary."

3. Write about three things you like and then about three things you do not like.

4. Remember that the lines should rhyme.

TIP: Try saying words out loud to get different effects.

5. Finish your rap by writing two lines about your hopes for your future.

6. Perform your rap with attitude!

I like rapping
It's so happ'ning!

Going Solo

Destiny's Child became the biggest-selling R&B girl group of all time. The group won countless awards and was recognized by the **National Association for the Advancement of Colored People** (NAACP) for presenting positive role models for young African Americans. At the annual NAACP Image Awards, Destiny's Child won the award for Outstanding Group five times between 2000 and 2006.

In 2001 Destiny's Child released *8 Days of Christmas*. From then on, the group members focused more and more on solo projects. During its 2005 *Destiny Fulfilled … and Lovin' It* tour, the group announced that it would split. All three singers remain very close friends, describing themselves as "sisters."

The NAACP

The National Association for the Advancement of Colored People is a U.S. **civil rights** organization. Its **mission** is to ensure there is equality between people and to eliminate **racial prejudice**.

In March 2006 Destiny's Child was awarded a star on the Hollywood Walk of Fame.

In 2004 Beyoncé sang the national anthem at the Superbowl in Houston.

A solo star

In 2001 Beyoncé released her first solo single, "Work It Out," from the movie *Carmen: A Hip Hopera*. She also began recording with other artists such as Marc Nelson and the rapper Jay-Z. She won a Grammy in 2004 for her duet "The Closer I Get to You" with Luther Vandross.

Beyoncé's voice has been described as a "superhuman instrument" owing to her ability to produce a wide range of emotions in her singing. As a mezzo-soprano, she can sing across at least three octaves, which is nearly half of the notes on a piano keyboard.

Solo success

In 2003 Beyoncé's first solo album, *Dangerously in Love*, went multi-platinum around the world. The hit singles "Crazy in Love" and "Baby Boy" are on this album. At the 2004 Grammy Awards, Beyoncé won five times and was the most successful artist at the awards that year.

A shy performer

Sometimes entertainers create a different identity on stage as a way of overcoming shyness or to tell stories. Musician David Bowie created a famous **alter ego** called Ziggy Stardust who dressed in a very **flamboyant** way and whose space adventures were told through songs. Beyoncé is quite shy and has said, "I come out of my shell when I'm on the stage." The confident performer Sasha Fierce is Beyoncé's alter ego when she is on stage.

Design a stage outfit

For her stage shows, Beyoncé dresses up and wears very striking outfits to help her become Sasha Fierce, and to allow her to be seen from a distance.

Steps to follow:

1. Get a large piece of paper, some colored pencils, colored paper, and pieces of material.

2. Think of a stage name for your superstar.

3. Is your star performing on a huge stadium stage or on a small studio stage?

4. Think about the image you want your superstar to project. It might be a glamorous, space age, or military look you want to create.

5. Draw the outline of a person.

6. Using the paper and material, cut out and paste the clothes onto the figure. Think about contrasting colors and textures for maximum effect.

7. Don't forget details like hair, makeup, and accessories.

8. Cut out your superstar and put it on display!

Acting the Part

Beyoncé turned her attention to Hollywood in 2002. She landed a role opposite Mike Myers in the comedy *Austin Powers: Goldmember* (2002). She played a character named Foxxy Cleopatra. The movie was a box office success around the world. Building on this, Beyoncé acted in another comedy, playing a singer in a remake of *The Pink Panther* (2006) opposite Steve Martin and Kevin Kline. She has said that she enjoys spending months with the same people when making movies because she can make friends, something she did not have time for as a child.

A girl's dream

Dreamgirls (2006) is a musical movie based on the history and development of R&B during the 1950s and 1960s. Beyoncé played the lead part of Deena Jones in the movie. Deena is a character based on Diana Ross, shown as a talented but shy singer who is manipulated by a **ruthless** manager, Curtis Taylor, Jr. Beyoncé earned two Golden Globe **nominations** for her performance.

Beyoncé played Foxxy Cleopatra in *Austin Powers: Goldmember*.

At the 2009 Oscars ceremony, Beyoncé performed a medley of songs with actor Hugh Jackman.

The supreme Diana Ross

One of Beyoncé's idols, Diana Ross, is an award-winning U.S. singer and actress. During the 1960s, she was the lead singer of The Supremes, before leaving the group for a solo career. Diana Ross was the first female solo artist to have six number-one hits. Over her career, Ross has recorded 61 albums and sold more than 100 million records. She is one of the few artists to have two stars on the Hollywood Walk of Fame: one for The Supremes and one as a soloist.

Private and public

In 2006, on her 25th birthday, Beyoncé released her second solo album, entitled *B'Day*. The album went straight to the number-one spot on the U.S. album charts and has gone multi-platinum. The song "Irreplaceable" was at the top of the U.S. charts for 10 weeks in a row. In the United Kingdom, the single "Déjà Vu" went to number one on the charts. Beyoncé toured the world in 2007 with *The Beyoncé Experience*. In the same year, Beyoncé became the first woman to win an International Artist Award at the American Music Awards.

A musical romance

In 2003 Beyoncé duetted with rapper Jay-Z on his song "03 Bonnie & Clyde." There were rumors of romance, but the couple always denied them. Since then, Beyoncé and Jay-Z have **collaborated** on many songs, including "Crazy in Love," "That's How You Like It," and "Upgrade U."

When she isn't working, Beyoncé likes to wear casual clothes and watch basketball with Jay-Z.

A very private couple

On April 4, 2008, Beyoncé and Jay-Z were married in New York City. There are no official or **paparazzi** photos of the day, and everyone who attended has kept the details of the wedding secret. It was five months later that Beyoncé first wore her wedding ring in public.

Meet Jay-Z

Jay-Z's real name is Shawn Carter. He is a rapper and **entrepreneur** (he starts and runs his own businesses). His music is extremely influential and popular. He has had 11 number-one albums in a row. Like Beyoncé, he has his own clothing line. He was in charge of Def Jam Recordings and helped found the record label Roc-A-Fella Records.

Making a Difference

Beyoncé makes regular contributions to charities and uses her fame to help good causes to raise money. With Kelly Rowland, Beyoncé has established the Knowles-Rowland Center for Youth, a multi-purpose community center in Houston.

In 2005 Beyoncé was made an ambassador for World Children's Day. The event takes place around the world on November 20 every year to raise money for children's charities. She released the song "Stand Up For Love," which became the anthem for the event.

Political change

The United States has a history of racial inequality. Barack Obama's presidential election campaign focused on the hope of changing this. Jay-Z campaigned for Obama in the run-up to the election. He encouraged African Americans and all young people to vote by thinking of earlier **civil rights** campaigners, saying: "Rosa Parks sat so Martin Luther King could walk. Martin Luther King walked so Obama could run. Obama is running so we all can fly." Beyoncé described Obama's **inauguration** as "the most important day of my life."

Here Beyoncé is painting pottery with a girl in a hospital in Washington, D.C., as part of her charity work.

In 2003 Beyoncé performed with Bono in South Africa to raise money for the fight against AIDS.

World of influence

Beyoncé has credited Michael Jackson with being an inspiration for her artistically. In turn, Beyoncé has influenced many young singers, such as Rihanna. Beyoncé says her goal is to inspire all young girls to achieve their dreams.

Destiny fulfilled?

In 2008 Beyoncé released her album *I Am … Sasha Fierce*. The album has sold millions of copies around the world and won MTV awards. At the Grammy Awards ceremony in 2008, Beyoncé performed a duet with Tina Turner, one of her musical inspirations. They sang Tina's hit "Proud Mary." Nearly a year in length, the 2009–10 *I Am …* tour saw Beyoncé perform more than one hundred concerts on six continents.

Tina Turner

Like Jay-Z, Tina Turner is a stage name. Her real name is Anna Mae Bullock. The U.S. singer and actress was born in 1939, and her 50-year career has produced many hits, including "River Deep, Mountain High," "Private Dancer," and "What's Love Got to Do With It?"

Beyoncé loves to perform on stage.

In 2008 Beyoncé was given the award for Outstanding Contribution to the Arts at the World Music Awards.

A measure of success

Forbes business magazine is published twice a month. It is famous for its lists of the richest Americans. In 2009 *Forbes* listed Beyoncé as the fourth most powerful and influential celebrity in the world. She was also the highest-earning celebrity under the age of 30, earning more than $87 million in 2008–09.

Career control

With more music and movie projects in the pipeline, Beyoncé shows no signs of slowing down. With her songwriting and musical **collaborations**, Beyoncé has gradually taken more control of her career. She makes the decisions about whom she works with and how she looks. The future looks bright for the multi-talented Beyoncé.

Timeline

1981	Beyoncé Giselle Knowles is born in Houston, Texas, on September 4
1988	Enters and wins first talent show, singing John Lennon's "Imagine"
1990	**Auditions** for and becomes a member of Girl's Tyme
1992	Girl's Tyme appears on *Star Search* but does not win
1993	The Taylor sisters and Tamar Davis leave Girl's Tyme while LeToya Luckett joins
	Girl's Tyme changes its name to Destiny's Child
1995	Mathew Knowles begins managing the group
1997	Destiny's Child signs with Columbia Records and releases its first song, "Killing Time"
1998	Destiny's Child releases its first album
1999	*The Writing's on the Wall* album is released
2000	The Destiny's Child song "Independent Women Part I" appears on the **soundtrack** to the movie *Charlie's Angels*
2001	Beyoncé appears in the musical movie *Carmen: A Hip Hopera*
	The Destiny's Child song "Say My Name" wins two Grammy Awards
	The album *Survivor* is released
2002	Beyoncé co-stars in the comedy *Austin Powers: Goldmember*, opposite Mike Myers

2003	Beyoncé releases *Dangerously in Love*, her first solo album
	Beyoncé sings on Jay-Z's hit single "03 Bonnie & Clyde"
2004	Beyoncé wins five Grammy Awards
	Destiny Fulfilled is released in November
	The House of Deréon fashion line is launched
2005	The members of Destiny's Child go solo
	Beyoncé and Kelly Rowland set up a charity called the Survivor Foundation
2006	Beyoncé lands a lead role in the movie *Dreamgirls* and co-stars in the movie *The Pink Panther*
	Destiny's Child is awarded a star on Hollywood's Walk of Fame
2007	*People* magazine votes Beyoncé the best-dressed celebrity
2008	Third solo album *I Am … Sasha Fierce* is released
	Beyoncé and Jay-Z marry in New York City
	At the World Music Awards, Beyoncé is given the award for Outstanding Contribution to the Arts
	Beyoncé stars as Etta James in the movie *Cadillac Records*
2009	Beyoncé sings at Barack Obama's **inauguration**
2010	Beyoncé is listed second on *Forbes* magazine's list of 100 Most Powerful and Influential Celebrities

Glossary

alter ego different personality or identity

audition performance in which a person tries out for a place in a group, or when a band tries to get a recording contract

breach of contract when a contract that has been signed between two people or companies is broken

choreography planning of dance moves

civil rights equality between people and an end to racial prejudice. The civil rights movement was particularly strong in the United States in the 1960s.

collaborate work with someone else

contract written agreement. A recording contract is made between an artist and a recording company to set out what has been agreed upon—for example, how many albums will be recorded.

entrepreneur person who starts and runs his or her own business

flamboyant brightly colored and attention-grabbing

icon very famous role model

inauguration ceremony to swear the U.S. president into office

mission special task

National Association for the Advancement of Colored People U.S. civil rights organization that works for equal opportunities for African Americans

nomination when a person or group is put forward as a candidate for an award

opening act group that plays before the main act at a concert

paparazzi photographers who follow famous people in the hope of finding a story

performing art art form that is presented on a stage, such as singing, dancing, or acting

racial prejudice disliking someone just because of his or her race

regime strict timetable

ruthless mean or cruel

signature song song that a person or group is famous for singing

soundtrack music that is in a movie

Find Out More

Books

Hodgson, Nicola. *Beyoncé Knowles* (Star Files series). Chicago: Raintree, 2006.

Destiny's Child albums

Destiny's Child (1998)

The Writing's on the Wall (1999)

8 Days of Christmas (2001)

Survivor (2001)

Destiny Fulfilled (2004)

Beyoncé albums

Dangerously in Love (2003)

B'Day (2006)

I Am … Sasha Fierce (2008)

Movies

Austin Powers: Goldmember (2002)

The Pink Panther (2006)

Dreamgirls (2006)

Cadillac Records (2008)

Place to visit

Destiny's Child's star on the Hollywood Walk of Fame, Los Angeles, California

Index